—QUICK START GUIDE—

THINK, ACT, BREATHE GLOBAL
And Grow Your Business

By Vernon Darko

Copyright ©2010 by Vernon D. Darko

P.O. Box 890131

Houston, TX 77289

Tel: 281.286.1338. | Fax: 281.286.2825

www.vernondarko.com

ISBN: 9781450576222

Printed and bound in the
United States of America

FOREWORD

I know from personal experience that tapping into the global market can be an intimidating experience due to language barriers, differences in culture and other various reasons. However, I am more than confident that Think, Act, Breathe Global will assist you in overcoming some of the foremost apprehensions and hurdles in dealing with foreign markets.

 Lack of knowledge in the global market is the number one reason that businesses remain limited, ultimately resulting in missed opportunities in foreign territories. This book is designed not only to fulfill that lack, but also to help overcome your fears, anxieties and doubts. Think, Act, Breathe Global is an excellent tool to increase knowledge and professionalism in the global market. You will obtain the confidence, strength, and the strategy to expand your borders and step out of your comfort zone into new and unchartered territories.

This book was written to suggest techniques and to give examples which demonstrate that your business doesn't have to be limited by remaining local or even national. With strategy, discipline, application and diligence, change in your business will become more and more evident. The techniques outlined in this book will give you the courage to step out and take advantage of not only cross-border commerce, but also the benefits, incentives, and the rewards involved for you, your business and the economy of that country causing a win-win situation for all. If you're ready to capitalize on this opportunity, then let's get started.

INTERESTING FACTS

UNITED STATES

U.S. Population – over 300 million (as of 2006 – growth rate 1.3% per year)

AFRICA

African Population – over 900 million (as of 2005 – 14% of the world's human population)

1. Africa is the world's second largest and second most populous continent after Asia.

2. The last 40 years have seen a rapid increase in population; hence, this population is somewhat young in comparison.

SOUTH AMERICA

South American Population – over 371 million (as of 2005 – with a land area covering 3.5% of the Earth's surface)

1. South America ranks fifth in population (after Asia, Africa, Europe and North America).

2. South America has an area of 6,890,000 square miles, ranking fourth in area (after Asia, Africa, and North America).

EUROPE

European Population – over 728 million (as of 2005 – more than 1/9 of the world's population)

1. It is the world's third most populous continent.

2. European demography continues to make major contributions in understanding international relations.

ASIA

Asian Population – almost 4 billion (as of 2005 – 60% of the world's population)

1. Asia is the world's largest and most populous continent.

2. It covers 8.8% of the earth's total surface area (or 29.4% of its land area)

Source: http://en.wikipedia.org

INTRODUCTION

When I first created Think, Act, Breathe Global and Grow Your Business, all I had was a twenty page self-published guide with my topics at the top and note pages that were passed out whenever I spoke at a seminar. I found this to be an excellent way to convey ideas; and through feedback received from successful attendees, I was informed that they ended up using what I provided like a workbook. In this Quick-Start Guide, I have decided to run with what worked for these successful entrepreneurs and business people and include a comprehensive reference tool which should help simplify Think, Act, Breathe Global into the essentials. These worksheets will help you with your planning and research.

ABOUT THE CHAPTER BY CHAPTER INFORMATION

Each chapter in Think, Act, Breathe Global contains a great deal of information. Instead of trying to take notes, these chapter worksheets will help you answer the questions which come up in each chapter. After the chapter worksheets, there are two worksheets designed to be printed in multiples to help assist you with specific countries and product research tasks that take into account all the chapters in this book.

TABLE OF CONTENTS

How To Research And Identify A Need In A Foreign Country
CHAPTER 1.

Your goal in this chapter is to identify a Need in a foreign country. If you are reading this book, you have likely already considered expanding outside of your nation. This section will help identify strengths and weaknesses in your plans and help expand on the notion of exporting.

There are three types of products which businesses provide to their consumers and clients: Goods, Services and Projects. Some quick definitions:

- Goods – Any tangible product that can be sold. Examples of goods that may be sold include automobiles, commodities, clothing, equipment and electronics.
- Service – Anything that does not require a tangible item or product. Examples of services include consulting, data processing, legal services, insurance and financial services.
- Projects – Involves more assets, methodical planning, engineering, fabrications and organization that are usually long term in nature. Projects combine both goods and services to accomplish a particular broad goal. Examples of projects include building refinery plants, factories, hospitals, hotels and real estate.

What are you considering taking global? Is it a Good, Service or Project?

_____

Describe the business you are considering taking global:

_____
_____
_____

Identify a Product to Take Global

How many different products are involved in your business? For instance, how many different goods, services or project types do you currently sell or work with?

_____
_____
_____

Now, what is the CORE of your business? Pick the top three selling products, services or projects that your company truly specializes in OR the ones that you think will be best exported. List them here:

_____   _____
_____   _____
_____   _____

Identify the Foreign Market

Are there foreign markets that you know will benefit from your product? Have your current sales been augmented by an occasional international order?

List any nations that you KNOW will benefit from your business:

_____   _____
_____   _____
_____   _____

Now, list nations that you THINK would benefit:

_____   _____
_____   _____
_____   _____

Finally, list any nations that you HOPE could benefit:

_____   _____
_____   _____
_____   _____

Necessary Research for Your Product

While researching your products, you must answer the following questions*:

> *(Hint: Check with U.S. Commercial Services and the country's or countries' Chamber of Commerce to help answer these questions.)*

1. Is there a true need for your product in the countries that you want to export to?
2. While the need may be there, is there economic sustainability to afford the product now and going forward?
3. Is your target consumer the public sector, private sector or both?
4. Is there competition for the product within the market?   Is this competition foreign or domestic?
5. Can you establish yourself as the expert in the field?
6. If there is competition, how saturated is the market? Can you set yourself apart somehow to be an effective competitor?
7. Is there enough market share left to carve out a decent profit?

Note: please refer to the following detailed worksheets for each of the above subjects.

Exporting Rules and Regulations

CHAPTER 2.

You will need to learn the exporting rules and regulations for both your home country as well as the countries you are exporting to. Avoiding pitfalls will prevent loss of income; and possibly penalties for violating the regulations.

Product Classifications

Go to: http://www.census.gov/foreign-trade/schedules/b/ to find the classification code for your product. You will find restrictions and requirements for the products, if there are any, while searching.

Export Controls

1. Are there restrictions to bringing the product into the destination country?
   (visit www.export.gov to help determine this)
2. Are inspections required for the product(s)?
3. Is there an embargo on the country currently?

Trade Party Screening

These questions should be answered about anyone you are working with in the foreign country:

1. Are the person(s) you are dealing with in the destination country on one of the ten lists that would violate the Export Administration Regulations (EAR)?
2. Have you researched any restrictions in the destination country on government and public sector sales?
3. Can you meet the criteria as required?
4. List any hurdles that will require investment of time or money to overcome:

Awareness of Export Restrictions and Requirements

      A. Shipping Requirements to countries of interest

      B. License Requirements for products

      C. Inspection Requirements

      D. Documentation Requirements

Notes

_____

_____

_____

_____

_____

_____

_____

_____

_____

_____

_____

_____

_____

_____

_____

_____

_____

_____

_____

_____

Research the Language, Culture and Political Climate
CHAPTER 3.

The language, culture and political climate will affect whether or not you want to do business in a particular country and how you are going to approach the customers and agents in the country.

Language Research

While doing language research, you need to answer these questions:

1. What is the official language(s) of the countries you want to export to?

2. Do these countries have regional dialects that are important to be aware of?

3. Have you secured translation services?

4. Are you prepared to learn a new language if necessary?

Research the Business Climate, Customs and Values

Questions to answer while researching the business climate, customs and values:

1. Have you researched the business climate, custom and values of the countries you are considering?

2. Is there any specific behavior pattern that you will need to exhibit or modify to be successful in those countries?

3. Can you find someone to interview from that country? Be sure to note things of interest that you learn from that interview.

Political Climate

Questions to answer about the political climate of a nation:

1. Is the country at war?

a. What is the source of the conflict?

b. Is the conflict isolated to a region or is it countrywide?

2. Is the country you are researching a communist country?

3. How safe is the country?

4. If the country is in distress, can you still get financing and appropriate insurance?

Ability to Conduct Financial Transactions

Being able to move money around and complete transactions in your country of export must be researched. Otherwise, if this is not achievable, it could prevent an award of business in some countries.

The four questions you must answer are:

1. Can you wire money out of country?
2. Do the banks have sufficient foreign currency to trade?
3. Are the country's banks reputable?
4. What percentage of your profit can be moved out of country?

Notes

_____

_____

_____

_____

_____

_____

_____

_____

_____

_____

_____

_____

_____

_____

_____

_____

_____

_____

_____

Organize a Support Group of Companies

CHAPTER 4.

Your support group of companies is vital to your success in any foreign market. While you may not need every one of these services, you will find that most of them are going to be necessary at some point during the process of building a successful and profitable business overseas. As you find partners, note their information here. You may want to consider printing multiple blank sheets of this page to use for each vendor.

Manufacturer or Vendor:

_____

Transportation and Shipping:

Shipping: _____

Export/Import Company: _____

Transportation Services: _____

Freight Forwarding Company: _____

Insurance Company:

Insurance of the Product: _____

Financing Insurance: _____

Business Insurance: _____

Documentation Specialist Company: _____

Translation Services: _____

Real Estate: _____

Financial:

Banking: _____

Tax Preparation: _____

Financial Reporting: _____

Legal: _____

Advertising:

Online Advertising: _____

Offline Advertising: _____

Administrative Agencies: _____

Employment Agencies to help staff your office and provide temporary assistance:

_____

Communication Service Provider:

Telephone: _____

Mobile Services: _____

Internet Services: _____

Notes

_____

_____

_____

_____

_____

_____

_____

Find a Foreign Partner or Agent
CHAPTER 5.

To do business effectively, you will need a representative in that country that you place your trust in to handle your business' affairs while you are not there; in addition to someone that can help secure permits and such in your absence.

Building a Pool of Candidates

Places to find a pool of candidates:

1. Conferences that promote foreign trade

2. Networking and business referrals from your travels

3. Your support group (see Chapter Four)

4. Corporate Council of Africa or similar council for the region you wish to trade

5. Country's Chamber of Commerce

6. Embassy contact

Checking the Pool to Find the Perfect Match

Research and investigation is required to find the perfect person to become your agent or business partner.

These are the places to research:

1. Your country's embassy or consulate for that country

2. The agent's embassy or consulate in your country

3. For U.S. Residents, the U.S. Commercial Services and Export Import Bank both offer screening programs.

   Many developed nations offer similar services through branches of their government.

Notes

_____

_____

_____

_____

_____

_____

_____

_____

_____

_____

_____

_____

_____

_____

_____

_____

_____

_____

_____

_____

_____

_____

(optional but highly recommended)

Benefits of establishing an office in a foreign country:

1. Creates a presence in that country

2. Improves sales conversions

3. Office costs can be lower

4. Makes the country's government happy

Where to establish your business presence in the country:

1. Your office should be located in a city, preferably the capital city, where major international flights go in and out of the country.

2. Your office should be located near the National Embassy of your country of origin.

3. Your office should be located in a business district or other area associated with the business you are in.

Instead of establishing your own business, partner with an established business that operates out of that country.

There are a number of benefits to this:

1. Skips the red tape and ground work

2. Mentoring

3. Better and quicker relationship formation

Notes

Take Advantage of Incentives Provided By Exporting To A Foreign Country
CHAPTER 7.

With a little research, finding incentives for doing business in your chosen country can yield big benefits and could sway your decision about which country to choose to export to.

These incentives come from three sources:

1. Your country of origin/country of domicile

2. The international community

3. The host country

U.S. programs for residents include (many developed countries have similar programs):

1. U.S. Export/Import Bank helps provide financing for foreign customers.

2. U.S. OPIC (Overseas Private Investment Corporation) offers business loans, grants and business services to people wanting to invest in specific countries around the globe.

International community programs are all done through the World Bank and the associated International Finance Corporation.

Host Country Incentives:

1. Land benefits

2. Financial transaction benefits

Notes

Take Advantage of Tax Incentives for Exporting
CHAPTER 8.

There are three types of Tax Incentives when working with an exporting business:

1. Tax incentives to assist with getting the product to the country.

2. Tax incentives to assist with getting the product INTO the country.

3. Other, more general business incentives.

Finding Tax Incentives:

1. Your nation's embassy or consulate in the destination country.

2. Your support group of businesses.

Notes

Take Advantage of Trade Financing

CHAPTER 9.

Trade financing allows you to use other financial resources in order to conduct business when exporting to another country. Without trade financing you may find that your ability to export is greatly curtailed.

Trade Financing Instruments:

1. Documentary Credit – Bank loans money to the importer and pays the exporter.

2. Counter Trade – Trade of goods in equitable amounts between exporter and importer.

Government Assistance:

Many countries offer trade financing subsidized by the government in order to encourage trade and boost the economy. For example, the Export/Import Bank of the U.S. can help insure and guarantee loans.

Notes

Travel to Enhance your Business
CHAPTER 10.

You will have to travel to visit the countries that you are building your business in. This is unavoidable.

The benefits of traveling to partner countries are:

1. When you travel to foreign countries it allows you to interact with your foreign clients helping you to establish and maintain solid relationships.

2. It allows you to put a face to a name when it comes to your business associates.

3. You can get a feel for foreign partners to ensure they are authentic and have your best interests at heart.

4. You can interact with employees to further instill a sense of loyalty to the business.

5. You can personally deal with any issues that arise ensuring the problems are addressed in a timely manner.

6. You can evaluate the daily operations of the business and gain greater insight on how improvements can be made.

7. It allows you to increase your customer base and your market by allowing you to personally network with clients.

8. A client or business partner is more liable to trust you when they have one on one interaction in person.

Tips to Maximize your Travel Time:

1. You will likely meet other business people in your travels. Use this opportunity to network.

2. Introduce yourself to others and initiate conversations. You never know where you might find a valuable employee, business partner, vendor or even a customer.

3. Conduct work while traveling.

4. Reply to any outstanding emails or written correspondence.

5. Catch up on industry reading.

6. Review your business plan and note how you may want to make changes for future growth. Start making notes now so you are prepared for later.

7. Plan the week, month or year ahead.

8. Use the time traveling to market yourself.

9. Brush up on the country's culture.

10. Use the time to study the language of the country.

11. Pack a pen and pad of paper.

12. Make sure you have a business mindset for your trip.

13. Fill your day with meetings and activities pertaining to work.

Tips to Save Money While Traveling on Business:

1. Don't fly first class.

2. Check with the refund policies of multiple airlines.

3. If you can schedule your time wisely, you may not mind the added time spent for connecting flights.

4. Shop around for your flights and compare round trip against two single one way flights.

5. Book your flight in advance.

6. Try to have as much flexibility in your travel schedule as possible.

7. Negotiate corporate rates with hotel chains.

8. Stay at hotels that are not in the center of the city.

9. Corporate housing can often offer discounts that are far better than a full service hotel.

10. Use public transportation when possible.

11. Consider alternate modes of travel especially when traveling from one country to another on an extended trip.

Notes

_____

_____

_____

_____

_____

_____

_____

_____

_____

_____

_____

The Importance of Customer Service

CHAPTER 11.

Excellent customer service is tantamount to success. Implement a plan from the beginning to make sure that you do not intimidate the first customers you get. In brief, these are the keys to making sure you are successful with offering proper customer service:

1. **Even if you are first to a market, make sure you are the best.**

   Competition will happen and if your customer service is lacking, you will become a target for the competition.

2. **Employees are the backbone of your company.**

   Satisfied, well trained employees that are allowed to make suggestions will provide better results.

3. **Keep Customer Communication professional but friendly.**

   Always use proper etiquette, regardless of communication means. Use proper language to instil customer confidence.

4. **Establish a complaint resolution process by listening to your customer and being proactive in resolving the issue.**

5. **Know your customer by gathering feedback and offer improvements such as extending existing customers usable incentives.**

6. **Establish a "Satisfaction Guaranteed" policy.**

Notes

Deliver on Time, Every Time

CHAPTER 12.

Even if the country you are exporting to does not expect timely delivery, it is still important to deliver on time, every time. Meeting and exceeding expectations is important and will result in repeat business.

Key concepts:

1.   **Deliver everything on time.**

From quotes to customer queries to the product itself, make sure it is there when you say it

will be or sooner.

2.   **Follow up with customers.**

3.   **Even if the country's culture does not value timeliness, deliver on time to exceed their expectations.**

4.   **Be aware of the time differences between countries.**

5.   **Be aware of the major holidays in the country or countries you are exporting to.**

Work Efficiently to Promote Timely Delivery.

Your time is important and valuable and if you can find ways to work smarter, you won't have to work harder to make sure that timely delivery happens. The ways to do this are:

1. Time management

2. Get organized

3. Prioritize

4. Be aware of constraints

5. Delegate whenever you can

6. Make sure your office is conducive to working

7. Find and utilize time management and project management tools

8. K.I.S.S. – Keep It Short and Simple

9. Evaluate and improve

Notes

_____

_____

_____

_____

_____

_____

_____

_____

_____

_____

_____

_____

_____

_____

_____

_____

Establishing & Maintaining Relationships
CHAPTER 13.

Relationships in business are integral to making sure that your business is successful. In some countries, you will not even get a foot in the door business-wise, until you have established a relationship with people in that country.

Building solid business relationships can be with:

1. Employees

2. Agents, Business Partners and Vendors

3. Customers and Clients

Keys to establishing relationships:

1. Communicate effectively and clearly

2. Go the extra mile

3. Be honest in your dealing with people

4. Be fair

5. Do what you say

6. Make sure the relationship is mutually beneficial

Notes

GOING GLOBAL

Country by Country & Product Research Worksheets

Country by Country Worksheet

Country of Focus: _____

Time Difference between your time zone? _____

Primary Language: _____

Secondary Language and Regional Dialects: _____

Government Type (Democracy, Theocracy, Communism, Dictatorship, etc.): _____

Is the Country Stable? _____. If no, what is the cause of the instability?

_____

_____

How Safe is the Country? _____

Can I Legally Travel Directly to This Country? _____

Is this country currently the subject of a trade embargo? _____

Culture Information:

Customs that need to be adhered to that differ from your own: _____

_____

Interview Notes: _

_____

_____

Financial Information

Can you get financing and insurance for business dealings within this country? _____

Can you Wire Money Out of Country? _____

Do the Banks have sufficient Foreign Currency to Trade? _____

Are the Country's Banks Reputable? _____

What Percentage of Your Profit can be Moved Out of Country? _____

Support Group of Companies

Have you secured all of the Support Group Companies and individuals necessary to do business in this country?

_____

List, then cross off as you find, any assets that you are missing: _____

_____

_____

_____

_____

Foreign Partner or Agent?

Candidates for Foreign Partner or Agent: (Circle the One You Choose)

_____

_____

_____

_____

_____

_____

Establishing an Office

What is your timeline for opening an office? In other words, during what phase of your business venture are you planning on opening your office in this country? _____

_____

Have you decided on a City or Region to build your office in? _____.

Note where that is once you have decided:

_____

In Lieu of an office, have you found a foreign business to partner with? _____

Note the business name: _____

Incentives for Doing Business in This Country

List any/all non-tax related incentives for doing business with this country:

_____   _____   _____

_____   _____   _____

_____   _____   _____

List any/all TAX related incentives for doing business with this country:

From The US: NO EXPORT TAXES _____

_____   _____   _____

_____   _____   _____

_____   _____   _____

_____   _____   _____

Product Research Worksheet

Product Basics:

From the Quick Start Guide, pick one of your products or services to research:

_____

_____

Briefly, what is your initial rationale for including this product? _____

_____

_____

_____

If there is a Supplier you use for this product, are they trustworthy? _____

Reliable? _____

What Countries are you considering exporting this product to?

_____	_____	_____
_____	_____	_____
_____	_____	_____
_____	_____	_____

NOTE: Be sure to fill out a Country worksheet for each of these countries.

Necessary Product Research:

1. Is there a true need for your product in the countries that you want to export to? _____

    Explain: _____

    _____

    _____

2. While the need may be there, is there economic sustainability to afford the product now and going forward? (In other words, are there enough people in the country that can afford your product?)

    _____

3. Is your target consumer the public sector, private sector or both? _____

    a. If your answer is public, or both, have you checked regulations for getting government contracts in the countries that you are wanting to export to?

    _____

4. Is there competition for the product within the market? _____

    _____

a. Is this competition foreign or domestic? _____

b. Can you establish yourself as the expert in the field? _____

c. How? _____

_____

5. If there is competition, how saturated is the market? _____

a. Can you set yourself apart somehow to be an effective competitor? _____

b. How? _____

c. Is there enough market share left to carve out a decent profit? _____

Exporting/Importing Information:

Product Classification Code: _____

Note any special licensing requirements or restrictions on the product: _____

_____

_____

_____

_____

Are there restrictions on the export of the product? _____

Are any of your listed countries on the restricted or banned list? _____

List them here:

_____

_____

_____

_____

_____

Are inspections required for the product? _____

Notes

Notes

www.ingramcontent.com/pod-product-compliance
Lightning Source LLC
Chambersburg PA
CBHW081241170526
45165CB00009B/3138